Linking art to the world around us

Arty Facts

Structures,
Materials,
& Art Activities

Crabtree Publishing Company
www.crabtreebooks.com

Crabtree Publishing Company

PMB 16A, 350 Fifth Avenue, Suite 3308
New York, NY
10118

612 Welland Avenue
St. Catharines, Ontario
L2M 5V6

Coordinating Editor: Ellen Rodger
Project Editors: P.A. Finlay, Carrie Gleason
Production Coordinator: Rosie Gowsell
Proofreading, Indexing: Wendy Scavuzzo

Project Development and Concept Marshall Direct:
Editorial Project Director: Karen Foster
Editors: Claire Sippi, Hazel Songhurst, Samantha Sweeney
Researchers: Gerry Bailey, Alec Edgington
Design Director: Tracy Carrington
Designers: Flora Awolaja, Claire Penny, Paul Montague,
James Thompson, Mark Dempsey,
Production: Victoria Grimsell, Christina Brown
Photo Research: Andrea Sadler
Illustrator: Jan Smith
Model Artist: Sophie Dean

Prepress, printing and binding by Worzalla Publishing Company

Cataloging in Publication Data
Taylor, Barbara, 1954-
   Structures, materials & art activities / Barbara Taylor.
   p. cm.
   ISBN 0-7787-1141-2 (pbk.) -- ISBN 0-7787-1113-7 (reinforced library binding)
   1. Handicraft--Juvenile literature. I. Title.
   TT157 .T388 2002
   745.5--dc21

                                        2002001323
                                           LC

Created by
Marshall Direct Learning

© 2002 Marshall Direct Learning

FRONT COVER IMAGES: DAVID TOMLINSON/ BRUCE COLEMAN COLLECTION, D. & J. HEATON/ SPECTRUM COLOUR LIBRARY; JEREMY HORNER/ CORBIS

Linking art to the world around us

Arty Facts

Structures, Materials, and Art Activities

Contents

WRITTEN BY Barbara Taylor

Stained glass

The glass of a window is hard, flat, and **transparent**. Amazingly, it is made from a mix of ingredients that you can find on a beach. Glass is made from sand, quartz, soda ash, and limestone. When these substances are heated together and then cooled, they make glass.

Colors from metals

People have been making glass this way for centuries. The ingredients are heated in large vats, or tanks, where they become transparent liquid glass. The liquid is either left clear, or it can be stained, or colored, by adding ground metals or chemicals. The metal cobalt gives glass a brilliant blue color. Red glass is made by adding the metals gold, copper, or selenium. Green glass can be made using the metal chromium.

Pictures in glass

Colored glass is often used in windows. These windows are usually made by skilled artists. The artist must cut the pieces of colored glass and arrange them in a picture or pattern. The glass pieces are then welded together using **molten** lead strips. Some of the most beautiful colored glass is found in the stained glass windows of churches and **cathedrals**.

When the sun shines through this stained glass window, pools of colored light fill the room.

Materials

WHAT YOU NEED

black poster board

light-colored pencil crayon

scissors

tape

colored tissue paper

glue

1 Draw an outline of a pattern of shapes on a piece of black poster board.

2 Cut out the shapes, leaving a frame around each.

3 Glue colored tissue paper behind the spaces in each frame.

4 Tape your pattern onto a window, so that the light shines through.

For a neater finish, use a craft knife. Ask an adult to help you.

Make your own colorful window designs

Hot wax

When we want light, we just flick a switch. Before electricity was invented, wax candles were the main source of light for most people. Candles were used as light and as a way of telling time in Egypt as far back as 5,000 years ago. When the wax melted to a point on a scale carved into the candle, they knew how much time had passed.

Flames of gas

A candle is a block of wax with a piece of string running through it. The string is called the wick and it sticks out at the top of the candle. As the wick burns, heat from the flame melts the wax at the base of the wick. The heat causes the liquid wax to flow up the wick and turn into a gas.

Wax and seals

Worker bees make wax to build the walls of the six-sided cells in their honeycomb. The wax comes from special glands under their **abdomens**. To collect beeswax, we gather honeycombs, remove the honey, then melt it. The melted wax is then strained to remove dirt and poured into molds until it sets. We use beeswax as a modeling material and to make candles. It is also used in furniture and floor waxes, waxed paper, and **ointments**. In the past, wax was used for seals, or wax stamps, that were used to close a letter or document. The wax was held over the paper and melted with a candle. A design was then pressed into the soft drops of wax. As the wax cooled, it hardened, holding the envelope or sheets of paper together. The seal was only broken by the person the letter was addressed to.

Materials

large candle

sequins

needle

glue

glitter

paints and brush

Carved candle

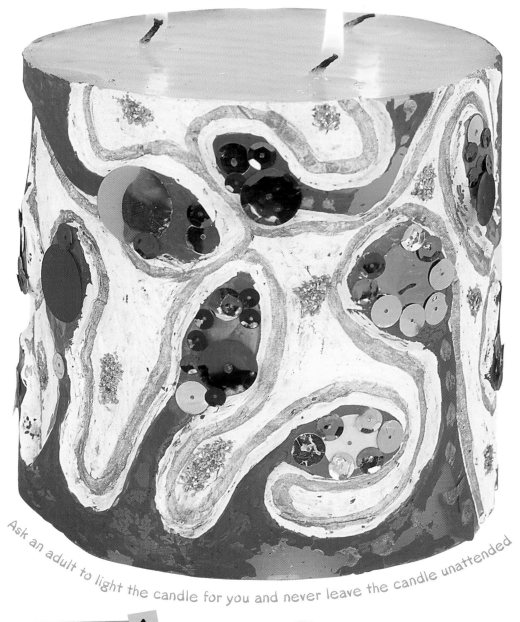

Ask an adult to light the candle for you and never leave the candle unattended

1 Carve a pattern on the candle with the needle or other carving tool.

Paint the candle and decorate the carved areas with sequins and glitter.

2

PVA

Pictures on walls

In some parts of the world, large, colorful pictures decorate the outside walls of buildings. In India and Egypt, paintings of gods, people, and animals make some streets look like giant picture books. Many old houses in Germany and Switzerland are painted with pictures from religious stories or folktales.

Cave paintings

Thousands of years ago, people in Europe, Africa, North America, and Australia painted pictures on the walls of caves. The pictures showed animals and hunters. These cave paintings were the first wall paintings, or murals. It is believed the caves were temples for celebrating successful hunting trips. The murals may have been used to bring good luck to the hunters on their trips.

Modern murals

People still paint pictures on walls. Murals are sometimes painted to brighten up a neighborhood, a playground, or a building. Colorful pictures of suns, trees, flowers, animals, and people can change a dull, ugly wall into a bright, interesting place.

Graffiti art

Rough drawings, writing, or marks on the walls of buildings are called graffiti. Scribbling on walls is nothing new. Ancient graffiti was found scrawled on the walls of Egyptian tombs and pyramids, Greek temples, and Roman buildings. Today, in many big cities, well-known graffiti artists cover the walls of public places with colorful art.

Frieze art

gold
thread

needle

poster
board

scissors

brush

black pencil
crayon

paints

1 Paint a
background
color on the
poster board.

2 Cut the poster
board into six small
pieces, all of the
same size.

3 Use a black pencil
crayon to draw
pictures on each panel,
such as people waking
up, feeding animals,
drawing, and reading.

Draw and paint other scenes to add to your frieze

Pin your frieze to
the wall. How long
can you make it?

4 Sew each panel
together with
gold thread to
create the frieze.

Tents and tipis

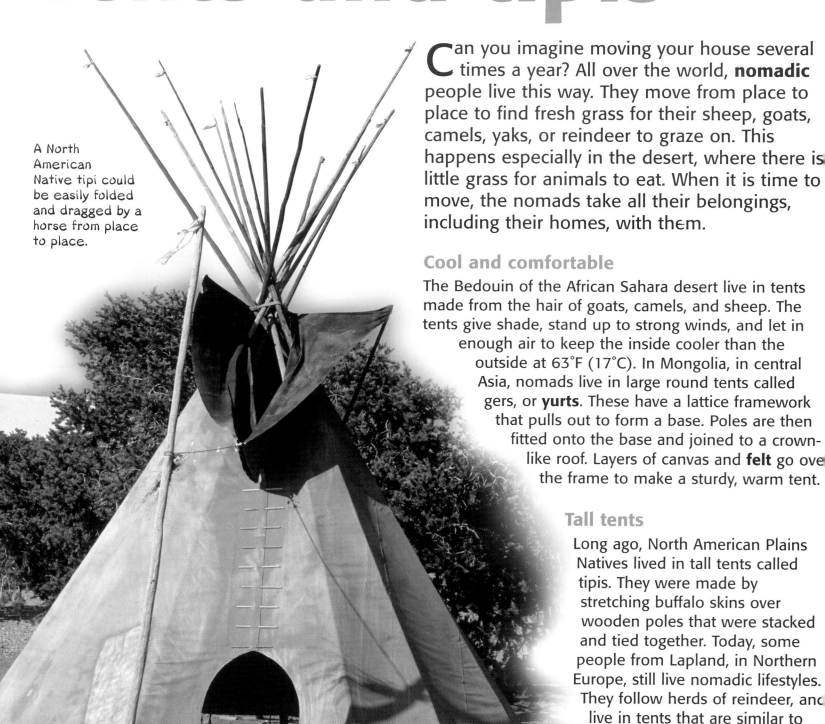

A North American Native tipi could be easily folded and dragged by a horse from place to place.

Can you imagine moving your house several times a year? All over the world, **nomadic** people live this way. They move from place to place to find fresh grass for their sheep, goats, camels, yaks, or reindeer to graze on. This happens especially in the desert, where there is little grass for animals to eat. When it is time to move, the nomads take all their belongings, including their homes, with them.

Cool and comfortable

The Bedouin of the African Sahara desert live in tents made from the hair of goats, camels, and sheep. The tents give shade, stand up to strong winds, and let in enough air to keep the inside cooler than the outside at 63°F (17°C). In Mongolia, in central Asia, nomads live in large round tents called gers, or **yurts**. These have a lattice framework that pulls out to form a base. Poles are then fitted onto the base and joined to a crown-like roof. Layers of canvas and **felt** go over the frame to make a sturdy, warm tent.

Tall tents

Long ago, North American Plains Natives lived in tall tents called tipis. They were made by stretching buffalo skins over wooden poles that were stacked and tied together. Today, some people from Lapland, in Northern Europe, still live nomadic lifestyles. They follow herds of reindeer, and live in tents that are similar to tipis called katas.

tructures

WHAT YOU NEED

clay

scissors

string

paper

pieces of fabric

sticks

glitter

glue

cellophane

paints and brush

1 Cut out semicircles of fabric and paint patterns on them.

2 Tie together five sticks and glue a semicircle of fabric around them.

3 To make the fire, scrunch up strips of paper into balls. Paint them and glue onto a circular piece of poster board.

4 Glue flame-shaped pieces of cellophane into the center of the poster board. Sprinkle on glitter.

5 To make logs, paint small rolls of paper brown and place around the fire.

6 Make people for your tipis. Use clay to make their heads and feet, string for their hair, and sticks for their bodies. Use pieces of fabric for their clothes.

Make and decorate other tipis for your camp

11

House of sticks

For thousands of years, people all around the world have lived in longhouses. A longhouse is a large house made from wood. It is usually big enough for a small community to live together. In Borneo, southeast Asia, a traditional longhouse can be as long as a street! As many as fifty families can live, cook, eat, and sleep inside one longhouse.

Building a longhouse

A longhouse is built using a row of wooden columns to hold up a central roof pole. Matching rows of columns form the walls on each side. The roof pole is joined to the wall beams by pieces of wood called **rafters**. The roof is covered with bundles of dried grasses or reeds.

The walls are made of clay, or **thatched** with grasses or reeds. In the past, some North American Natives used logs and tree bark to build longhouses, and Europeans used woven twigs plastered with clay.

Stilts and dome structures

People in Indonesia and Polynesia build longhouses that are raised above the ground on stilts to protect them from the floods in the rainy season. Each family has its own sleeping area and place to work. The rest of the house is one large room that everyone shares and uses for eating, playing music, and dancing. Until the nineteenth century, the Iroquois people of north-eastern North America lived in wood and bark longhouses. Their domed roofs were made by bending thin trees on one side over to the other side. This frame was then covered in bark. Cooking was done in the middle of the longhouse, where an opening in the roof was used as a chimney.

House on stilts

cardboard box

poster board

scissors

hay

string

popsicle sticks

toothpicks

glue

beach mat

corrugated cardboard

1 Cut window shapes and a door in the box. Cover the box, except for the flaps, with popsicle sticks.

2 Gather bunches of hay and tie each end with string. Glue them onto a piece of poster board and then glue the poster board onto the front flap of the box.

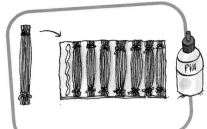

3 Make stilts by rolling up pieces of corrugated cardboard. Glue them to the bottom of the house. Glue popsicle sticks onto the stilts, as shown.

4 Glue popsicle sticks onto a piece of poster board to make a porch. Glue toothpicks to string to make a ladder.

5 Cut a rectangle and two triangular shapes from a beach mat, to make the sides and back of the roof. Glue them to the house and then glue the front roof, on a slant, to the sides.

Make cardboard cut-out people for your house

13

Bricks and mortar

People have been using bricks to build with for thousands of years. Six thousand years ago, the Egyptians made bricks from mud mixed with straw. They left them in the sun to harden, or baked them in a type of oven called a kiln. Even today, in hot countries, some people still use this method of making mud bricks to build their homes.

Designed for strength

Today, buildings can be made from many different materials. Buildings are **constructed** from steel, glass, plastic, or some other high-tech material. Many buildings are still built with bricks and **mortar** using traditional methods.

A home made of sun-baked mud bricks.

Bricklaying

Look closely at a brick wall to see how the bricks are arranged. Usually, they are placed in an overlapping pattern. Arranging the bricks like this gives the wall more strength. To increase the strength even more, the bricks are then stuck together with a layer of mortar. Mortar is made by mixing together cement, limestone, sand, and water.

Rough or smooth

Bricks can be made with many different surface textures ranging from smooth to rough. They also come in different colors, depending on the color of the material they are made from.

Builder's tools

Building brick walls takes a lot of skill. The walls need to be straight, otherwise the building will be unsafe and might collapse. Builders use special tools to help them construct the walls of buildings properly. A **plumb line** is a heavy weight on a string used to make sure the walls are vertical. A level is used to make sure the rows of bricks are horizontal. The bricklayer stacks the bricks in an open wooden box attached to a pole, called a hod, to carry them on a building site. A trowel is a tool used to spread the mortar that cements the bricks together. It is also used to tap the bricks firmly in place.

Materials

Building collage

scissors

crayons

poster board

colored construction paper

glue

pencil

1 Using crayons and paper, make rubbings of different surfaces inside and outside your home.

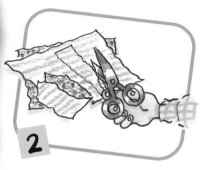

2 Draw shapes of buildings onto your rubbings and cut them out.

3 Glue the shapes onto the poster board to form a row of different buildings.

Design a street filled with all kinds of different buildings

15

Cities on water

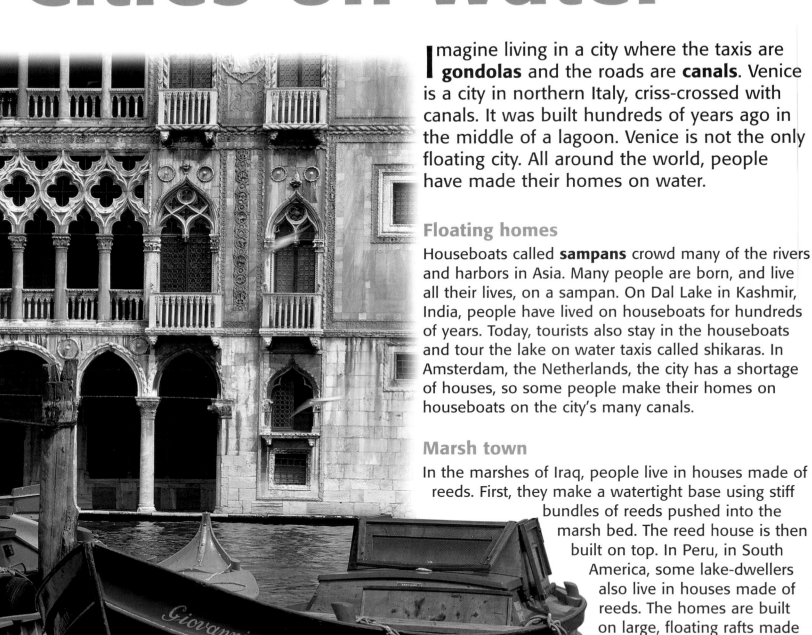

Imagine living in a city where the taxis are **gondolas** and the roads are **canals**. Venice is a city in northern Italy, criss-crossed with canals. It was built hundreds of years ago in the middle of a lagoon. Venice is not the only floating city. All around the world, people have made their homes on water.

Floating homes

Houseboats called **sampans** crowd many of the rivers and harbors in Asia. Many people are born, and live all their lives, on a sampan. On Dal Lake in Kashmir, India, people have lived on houseboats for hundreds of years. Today, tourists also stay in the houseboats and tour the lake on water taxis called shikaras. In Amsterdam, the Netherlands, the city has a shortage of houses, so some people make their homes on houseboats on the city's many canals.

Marsh town

In the marshes of Iraq, people live in houses made of reeds. First, they make a watertight base using stiff bundles of reeds pushed into the marsh bed. The reed house is then built on top. In Peru, in South America, some lake-dwellers also live in houses made of reeds. The homes are built on large, floating rafts made from reeds.

Venice has streets of water for gondola traffic as well as pavement for vehicle traffic.

Structures

Bridges and arches

What other structures can you make over water?

WHAT YOU NEED

- scissors
- poster board
- corrugated cardboard
- pencil
- glue
- glitter
- paints and brush

1 Paint a water scene on a piece of poster board and decorate with glitter.

2 On another piece of poster board, draw the outlines of small, medium, and large buildings. Paint and cut them out.

3 Cut out small squares of thick cardboard and glue them to the backs of the buildings. Glue these onto the water background scene to create a 3-D effect.

4 Draw a variety of arched bridges. Cut out and glue them onto the picture, using the technique in step 3 to create a 3-D effect.

17

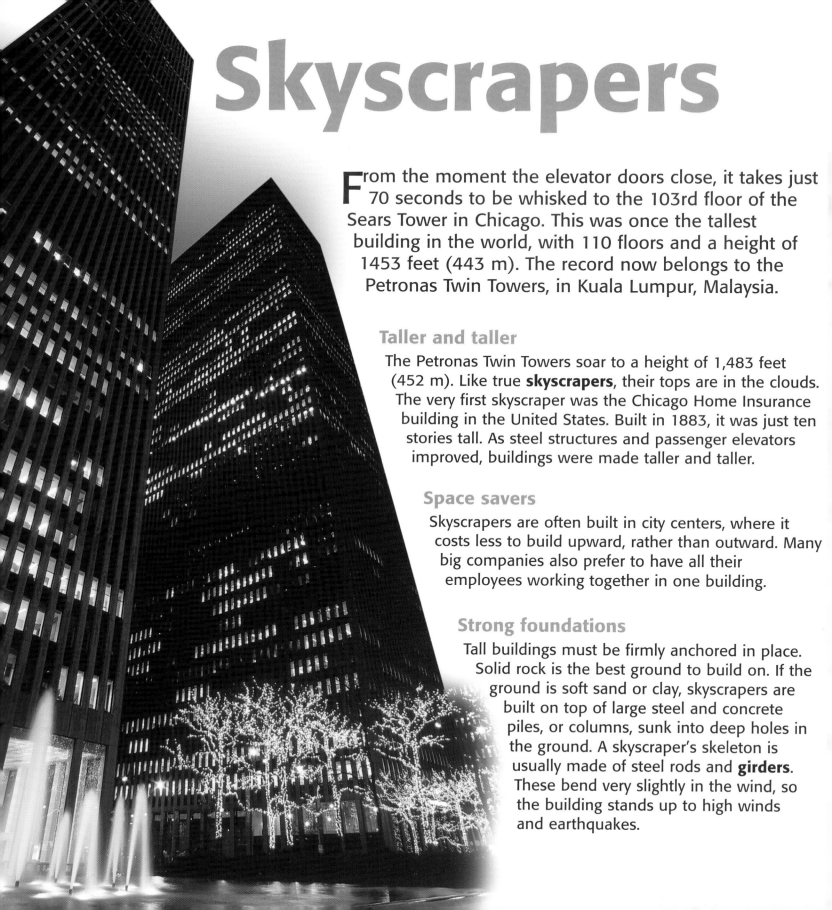

Skyscrapers

From the moment the elevator doors close, it takes just 70 seconds to be whisked to the 103rd floor of the Sears Tower in Chicago. This was once the tallest building in the world, with 110 floors and a height of 1453 feet (443 m). The record now belongs to the Petronas Twin Towers, in Kuala Lumpur, Malaysia.

Taller and taller

The Petronas Twin Towers soar to a height of 1,483 feet (452 m). Like true **skyscrapers**, their tops are in the clouds. The very first skyscraper was the Chicago Home Insurance building in the United States. Built in 1883, it was just ten stories tall. As steel structures and passenger elevators improved, buildings were made taller and taller.

Space savers

Skyscrapers are often built in city centers, where it costs less to build upward, rather than outward. Many big companies also prefer to have all their employees working together in one building.

Strong foundations

Tall buildings must be firmly anchored in place. Solid rock is the best ground to build on. If the ground is soft sand or clay, skyscrapers are built on top of large steel and concrete piles, or columns, sunk into deep holes in the ground. A skyscraper's skeleton is usually made of steel rods and **girders**. These bend very slightly in the wind, so the building stands up to high winds and earthquakes.

Fantasy downtown

variety of boxes

box lid

metallic paper

tin foil

long cardboard tube

tape

bottle cap

sequins

stick

poster board

glue

glitter

colored acetate

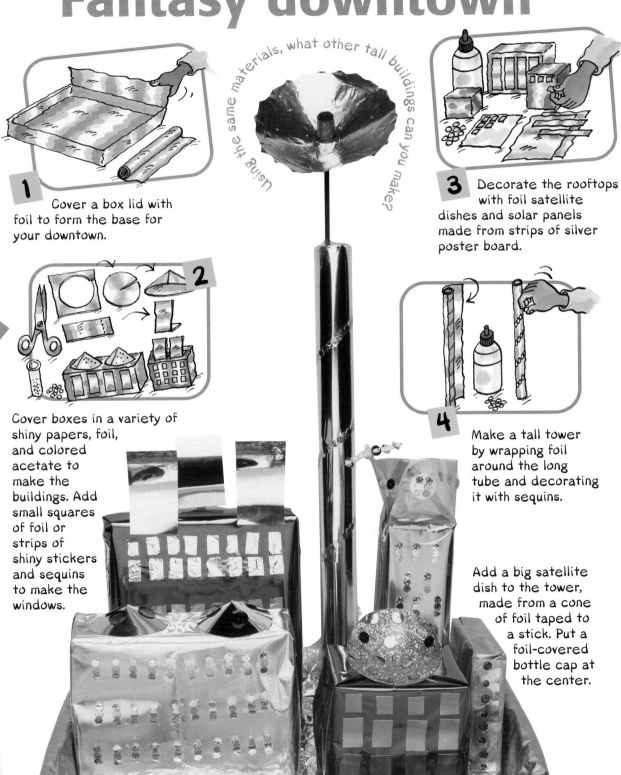

Using the same materials, what other tall buildings can you make?

1 Cover a box lid with foil to form the base for your downtown.

2 Cover boxes in a variety of shiny papers, foil, and colored acetate to make the buildings. Add small squares of foil or strips of shiny stickers and sequins to make the windows.

3 Decorate the rooftops with foil satellite dishes and solar panels made from strips of silver poster board.

4 Make a tall tower by wrapping foil around the long tube and decorating it with sequins.

Add a big satellite dish to the tower, made from a cone of foil taped to a stick. Put a foil-covered bottle cap at the center.

19

Crumbling columns

The ruins of the sanctuary of Athena at Delphi, Greece.

All over the world, you can find the ruins of ancient buildings. In Greece, for example, towering columns that were once part of magnificent Greek temples stand alone among crumbling ancient stones of an earlier time. These ancient, weathered structures tell us a story of how people lived thousands of years ago, of how they built their cities, palaces, and places of worship.

Ancient jigsaw

Archaeologists study the remains of past human cultures. When a site is found, these scientists dig, or excavate, carefully among the ruins for buried objects. It takes hours and hours of work, but gradually the archaeologists can piece together information about ancient times. Every object found, whether it is a piece of pottery or stones from an archway or temple, helps in understanding the people of an earlier culture.

Supports and frameworks

The ancient Greeks built many temples. They tried to achieve beauty and symmetry, or balance, in their buildings. The tall columns of a Greek temple surrounded a long, inner chamber. The columns gave the building its basic shape and design. Very thick walls were not needed. By evenly spacing the columns and placing them in rows, the building and roof were easily supported. Elaborate stone carvings added to the overall beauty of the building. In ancient times, constructing a building was a very hard and time-consuming process. Stone had to be carried long distances and carved by hand.

Structures

Greek ruins

1 Soften the clay and mold it into columns, a triangular arch, and bricks for loose rubble. Use the edge of the scissors to scratch textures into the columns.

2 Glue sand onto the top and sides of a cardboard box lid to make the base.

3 To make steps, cut a piece of poster board and fold it into steps. Paint, or glue on sand, then glue the steps to one of the long edges of the base.

Paint your clay pillars, arch, and bricks. Glue your arrangement into place on the base.

Make clay pots and statues to add to your ruins

21

Standing stones

Buried in the rainforests of Mexico and standing tall on Easter Island in the Pacific Ocean are mysterious, gigantic stone heads. They were made thousands of years ago by ancient peoples. Ancient circles of stones can be found in many parts of western Europe. The most famous of these is Stonehenge in southern England. Who built these strange stone monuments, and why?

Giant heads

The giant carved heads on Easter Island were made 400 to 1,000 years ago. They vary in height, from 10 to 40 feet (3 to 12 m), and some weigh more than 110,000 pounds (50 tons). They were carved from soft, volcanic stone and lifted into place using ropes, wooden **levers,** and piles of stones for support. The statues are thought to be of important people who became gods after they died. Other discoveries include stone jaguars and snakes in Mexico. They are the only evidence of the Olmec people who lived there 2,000 to 3,000 years ago.

The giant carved statues on Easter Island.

Sun temple?

The circle of large standing stones known as Stonehenge was built more than 4,000 years ago in southern England. We can only guess how the stones were carried, shaped, and placed upright. It is possible Stonehenge was a temple to the Sun, or an observatory, which is a place for tracking the movement of the Sun, Moon, and stars. The stones used to construct Stonehenge are even older than those of the pyramids of Egypt.

Structures

WHAT YOU NEED

clay

PVA glue

wire

brush

paints

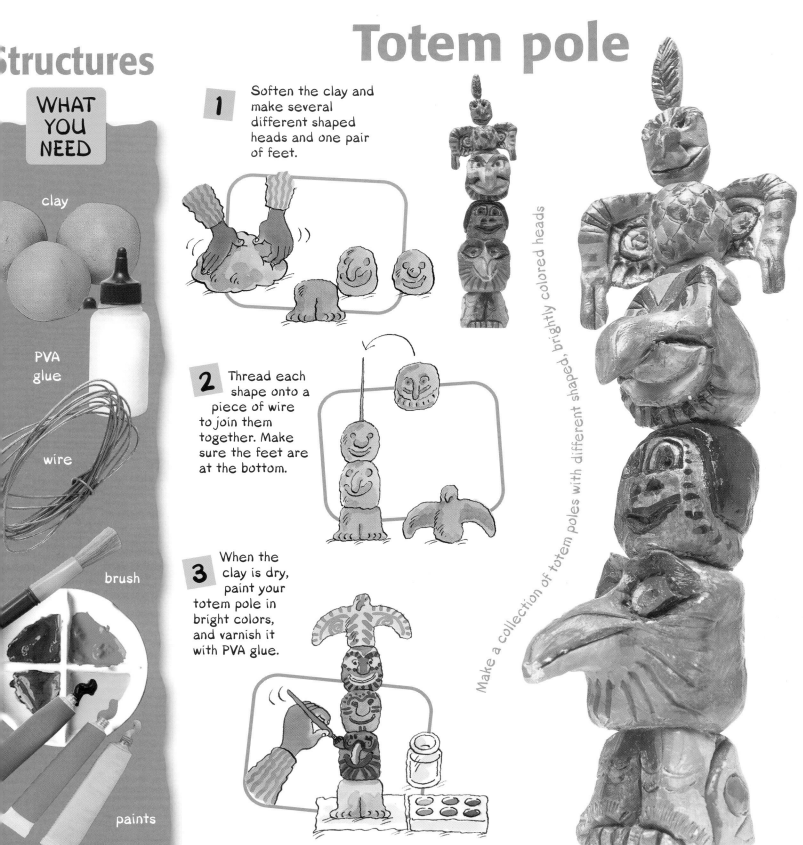

1 Soften the clay and make several different shaped heads and one pair of feet.

2 Thread each shape onto a piece of wire to join them together. Make sure the feet are at the bottom.

3 When the clay is dry, paint your totem pole in bright colors, and varnish it with PVA glue.

Make a collection of totem poles with different shaped, brightly colored heads

23

Mighty pyramids

Can you imagine building a pyramid with more than two million stone blocks, each weighing more than 4,400 pounds (2,000 kg)? The Great Pyramid at Giza in Egypt is this big. It was built about 4,500 years ago, as a tomb for Pharaoh Khufu. To guard against tomb robbers, the pharaoh's **mummified** body was laid in a secret chamber in the middle of the pyramid. Treasures were placed in the chamber for the king to use in the **afterlife**.

Muscle power

It took 20 years to build the pyramid at Giza. In ancient Egypt, the only building tools were simple copper chisels and saws, stone hammers, and wooden **squares**.

Instead of machine power, the Egyptians used the muscle power of hundreds of thousands of workers. They cut large blocks of stone from nearby **quarries** and pulled them across the sand on rollers or **sledges**

Sand and ramps

The pyramid's base was a perfect square, marked out with string and pegs. As the pyramid grew higher, giant slopes of sand were piled up on the sides. The stones were pulled up these sand ramps and workers are believed to have used levers to move the stones into their final positions. When the last block was in place, thousands of pounds of sand had to be cleared away. This sand is still piled around some pyramids today. To finish the pyramid, it was covered with dazzling white limestone to make it shine in the sun. No one is sure why the pyramids were triangle-shaped. People believe it may have been to give the pharaoh a stairway to the afterlife.

Pharaoh's tomb

styrofoam

sand

glue

scissors or craft knife
(Ask an adult for help when using a knife.)

white gauze

paints
and
brush

1 Draw a square and four equal triangles on the styrofoam. Cut them out.

2 With the scissors, carve brick shapes onto the four triangles.

3 Mix sand with paint and brush over the pyramid pieces. Glue three triangles to the square base.

4 Cut a long strip of styrofoam and make steps on it with the scissors. Paint and glue the steps to the fourth triangle. Make a small square hole at the top of this triangle and glue it to the model.

5 Cut out a cat god and a tomb from the styrofoam and paint them. Make a mummy out of clay and wrap it in gauze. Paint a square of styrofoam with hieroglyphics, or symbols.

Make some treasure out of beads and buttons to put in your pharaoh's tomb

Place mummies, treasures, and secret manuscripts inside your pyramid.

Floor art

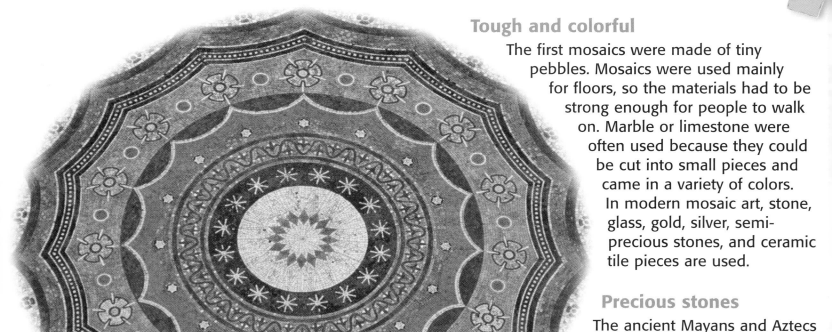

Tough and colorful

The first mosaics were made of tiny pebbles. Mosaics were used mainly for floors, so the materials had to be strong enough for people to walk on. Marble or limestone were often used because they could be cut into small pieces and came in a variety of colors. In modern mosaic art, stone, glass, gold, silver, semi-precious stones, and ceramic tile pieces are used.

Precious stones

The ancient Mayans and Aztecs of Mexico made beautiful mosaics from semiprecious stones. The stone turquoise was their favorite material, but they also used garnet, quartz, beryl, malachite, jadeite, and gold. Mosaics were used to decorate many items including masks, shields, and helmets.

Imagine doing a jigsaw puzzle with over 100,000 pieces! **Mosaics** are like jigsaw puzzles. They are designs made from thousands of tiny colored pieces. The pieces are small squares, triangles, or other shapes that fit closely together to make a pattern. Ancient Romans decorated floors, fountains, walls, and baths with beautiful mosaics.

Roman scenes

Roman mosaics showed gods and many kinds of scenes bordered by **geometric** shapes. The floor of an average room in a Roman house needed more than 100,000 mosaic pieces. Two or three layers of mortar, a kind of cement, was spread on a thick stone base to make just one mosaic. A sketch of the overall picture was drawn onto the base and the mosaic pieces pressed into place.

Structures

Mosaic

- lentils
- toothpicks
- sand
- beans
- colored glass pieces
- beads
- pebbles
- pencil
- popsicle sticks
- construction paper
- poster board
- glue

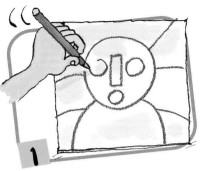

1 Draw the outline of a picture in pencil on construction paper.

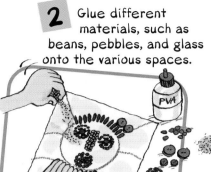

2 Glue different materials, such as beans, pebbles, and glass onto the various spaces.

3 Mount your mosaic picture on poster board.

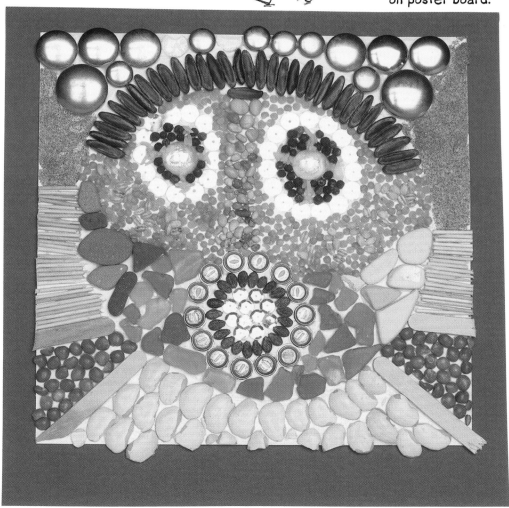

Make a gallery of mosaics for your bedroom wall

27

Castle towers

Most castles were built in the **Middle Ages** by wealthy people, such as lords or kings and queens. The castles were used as powerful fortresses as well as homes. With their strong walls and high towers, they were designed to keep out enemies. Most castles were built on a hill and surrounded by a **moat**. When the **drawbridge** over the moat was pulled up, the castle became an island stronghold, or fortress.

The gatehouse

The weakest part of a castle was the entrance. This was protected by thick doors, a tall gatehouse full of soldiers, and an iron gate called a **portcullis**. The portcullis guarded the castle entrance and was pulled up and down by special winding equipment in the gatehouse.

Walls and battlements

The **battlements** at the top of the castle walls had gaps for soldiers in the castle to fire arrows through. Narrow slits in the walls were perfect for firing arrows out, but too narrow to let enemy fire come in. Many castles also had stone **parapets** jutting out from the tops of the walls. Soldiers could drop heavy stones or boiling water and oil on top of attackers through holes in the parapets.

Enemy attack!

Soldiers kept a lookout for enemies who would climb up over the battlements using long ladders, or tall, wooden towers on wheels. To fight their way inside a castle, soldiers used giant **catapults** to hurl stone boulders at the walls. Large crossbows on wheels fired large, heavy **bolts**. Battering rams, or heavy wooden beams, were swung from chains, or rolled on wheels, to smash castle walls and doors.

Castle stronghold

WHAT YOU NEED

poster board

glue

paints and brush

scissors

string

toothpicks

popsicle sticks

ewspaper

blue tissue paper

2 Cut out three pieces of poster board to make the walls and entrance. Glue them to the towers to make the main part of the castle.

1 Cut slit windows and towers from two pieces of poster board. Roll the poster board into tubes and glue them to make two towers.

3 Glue popsicle sticks together to make the drawbridge. Paint, then glue them to the castle door. Paint the castle.

5 Glue scrunched-up newspaper to a large piece of poster board to make grass banks around a moat and a middle mound for the castle to sit on. Paint the base and cover the moat with blue tissue paper.

4 Glue toothpicks together into a grid to make a gate. Paint, then glue the gate inside the door. Make holes, and thread string through the drawbridge and entrance wall, so that your drawbridge can open and close.

Make flags to stick on the towers

Rooftops

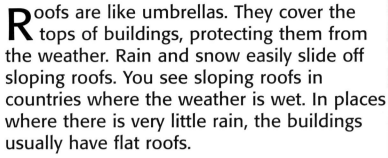

Roofs are like umbrellas. They cover the tops of buildings, protecting them from the weather. Rain and snow easily slide off sloping roofs. You see sloping roofs in countries where the weather is wet. In places where there is very little rain, the buildings usually have flat roofs.

Pagoda curves

Other roof shapes include tall, thin church spires, **domes**, and the tiered roofs on **pagodas**. Pagodas are a type of tower, with many stories, or tiers. Each tier has a decorated, overhanging roof that curves up at the edges. Many pagodas are places of worship, such as **Buddhist** temples.

Straw, tar, and tiles

The first roofs were probably made of straw, leaves, branches, or reeds. Thatched roofs of grasses are still used in some parts of the world. Flat roofs are usually covered with special roofing felt and tar. Sloping roofs have a wooden, concrete, or steel framework that is covered in sheets of corrugated metal, or tiles made from clay or slate.

Keeping warm

Roofs are often lined with a layer of material called **insulation** that has many air pockets. Since air traps heat, the insulation helps to keep a building warm in winter and cool in summer.

The layered roofs on this tall pagoda protect it from the sun's rays and the rain.

Rooftop gardens

oster oard

olored aper

glue

string

aints nd brush

toothpicks

scissors

tissue paper

cardboard boxes

1 Cut windows and doors from the cardboard boxes to make houses.

2 Cut small squares from red paper and glue onto a piece of poster board to make a tiled roof. Glue them onto the front of one house.

3 Paint your houses in bright colors.

Paint bottle tops to make flower pots for your rooftop garden

4 Fold a narrow piece of poster board into stairs. Glue the staircase onto one side of a house.

5 Make grass and flowers from green poster board. Glue string to make stems for your flowers.

6 To make people, cut heads from poster board and glue them to toothpicks. Use tissue paper for clothes.

Golden domes

All over the world, domes decorate the tops of important and beautiful buildings. The ancient Romans built them on temples such as the **Pantheon** in Rome. You can also see them on cathedrals, **mosques**, and tombs. Look for domes on top of other buildings as well, such as museums and even large stores. Some domes are plain, but many are gold, brightly colored, or even covered with richly patterned tiles.

World famous

The Mosque of Omar, in Jerusalem, is also called the Dome of the Rock because of its magnificent, dome-shaped golden roof. The Taj Mahal in India, the Florence Cathedral in Italy, and St. Basil's Cathedral in Moscow are other world-famous domed buildings.

Giant spaces

Domed structures are difficult to build, but they create large spaces inside buildings. Domes are built from triangular or many-sided pieces that spread out the weight of the structure. **Geodesic domes** are strong, lightweight, modern domes used for factories, sports stadiums, theaters, or exhibitions. They can be made of materials as varied as plastic or cardboard.

The spectacular domes of Ubadiah mosque in Kuala Kangsar, Malaysia.

Glittering domescape

paper

colored
poster
board

pencil

gold, sliver, and
metallic paper

pastels

glue

Glittering and shiny domes glistening in the moonlight

1 Draw an outline of domes on paper.

2 Use the pastels and metallic papers to color and make patterned domes.

3 Mount your picture on poster board.

33

Building bridges

The best way to cross a river, canyon, or other kind of obstacle is to use a bridge. A bridge saves you having to swim, take a boat, or travel a long way around the obstacle. A bridge can be a simple tree trunk laid across the water, or a massive suspension bridge that stretches hundreds of feet across a gorge.

Weight carriers

A bridge must be able to hold its own weight and the weight of all the traffic crossing it. A beam bridge, such as a wood plank laid across a stream, is the simplest kind of bridge. Each end is supported by the riverbank. Beam bridges are only good for connecting short distances. Arch bridges have a series of arches which carry the weight outward along two curving paths down to the ground. The Sydney Harbor Bridge in Australia is an arch bridge made of steel which has a span of nearly 1,650 feet (503 m).

Suspension bridges

A suspension bridge is a modern version of the simple rope bridge used by people for thousands of years. Most of the world's really large bridges, such as the Golden Gate bridge in San Francisco, are suspension bridges. The bridge hangs, or suspends, from thick steel cables strung between tall towers. The ends of the cables are anchored firmly on either side of the bridge. The cables carry the weight of the bridge and its traffic to the towers and then to the ground. The towers must be very strong and stuck firmly in the ground.

The Golden Gate bridge in San Francisco, California, stretches for 4,200 feet (1,280 m).

Canyon bridge

WHAT YOU NEED

buttons

sand

cardboard

string

poster board

newspaper

sponge

matchboxes

popsicle sticks

scissors

glue

paints and brush

1 Scrunch up newspaper and glue it to a large piece of poster board to make a canyon and river.

2 Paint the canyon. When it is dry, glue sand on it.

3 Glue popsicle sticks onto two pieces of string to form swing bridges. Glue the bridges over the river.

4 Cut pieces of sponge into bush and tree shapes. Paint and glue them onto your canyon.

Make model cars from matchboxes. Use buttons and cardboard circles for the wheels. Paint and decorate them.

What other materials can you use to make bridges?

Busy highways

Roads join villages, towns, and cities across all the countries of the world. They allow goods and people to be carried quickly and easily from place to place. Some roads are dirt tracks just wide enough for a single car. Others are big highways with many lanes and trucks, buses, and cars zooming along them at high speeds. In cities, highway interchanges form a tangle of busy roads crossing above, below, and around each other. Many people think building new roads is not good for the environment because it ruins animal habitats and encourages people to drive more.

Moving earth

New roads are often built across open countryside. The roadbuilders must find out what kind of soil and rock an area is made of. They also look at how much damage an area will suffer, and work out the cost of building the road. The route is then marked out, ready for the large, earth-moving machines.

Making links

The Romans built long straight roads, linking towns and cities in their empire, and enabling Roman troops to march quickly from place to place. The world's longest road joins the state of Texas with Valparaiso in Chile. It is more than 16,155 miles (26,000 km) long.

Cardboard highway

- scissors
- toothpicks
- plastic bottle
- newspaper
- clay
- corrugated cardboard
- glue
- poster board
- pencil
- paints and brush

1 Draw an outline of a road on a large piece of poster board.

2 Scrunch up newspaper and glue onto the poster board to make grassy hills. Paint your model.

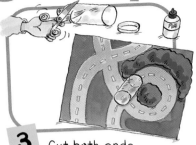

3 Cut both ends off a plastic bottle and glue it onto any part of the road.

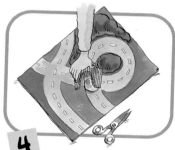

4 Cut out and paint a piece of corrugated cardboard and glue over the top of the bottle to make an overpass.

5 Draw, paint, and cut out road signs and trees. Stick each one on the end of a toothpick and use small pieces of clay as stands.

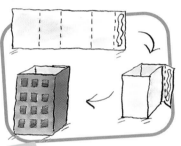

6 Add cardboard buildings or animal crossings to your road scene. Use model cars to drive on the winding roads.

Play a game of cars with your friends on your winding road model

Beacons of light

Sailing a ship close to shore at night has always been dangerous. There are often rocks, sandbanks, reefs, cliffs, or other unseen hazards. To help navigators steer their way safely, guiding lights warn of the dangers ahead. The sweeping beam from a lighthouse **beacon** lights up the night sky and the dark shore waters, guiding ships safely around the hidden dangers near shore.

Towers of light

Most lighthouses are simple towers made of brick, stone, wood, or metal. They are built on coastlines, on peninsulas, on rocks, in the sea itself, and at ports and harbors. Some lighthouses are solid towers. Others have a platform with a house-like structure on top. Some are no more than a metal frame with a light on top.

Flashes in the dark

In ancient times, lighthouses were lit by fire. Later, oil lamps were used. Today, lighthouses have a bright electric light and a special lens that revolves around the light, making it blink. Each lighthouse has its own pattern of blinking light.

Lighthouse soap dish

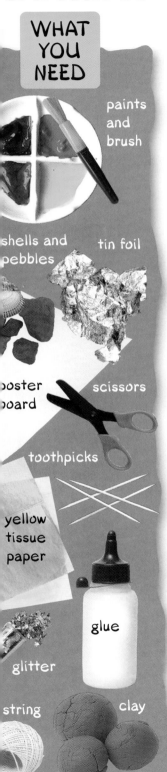
1

Roll a piece of poster board into a slim cone shape. Cut off the top and bottom, so the cone stands up. Cut out round windows and paint.

2 Soften the clay and make a rocky base around the lighthouse. Leave a shallow dip in the clay for your soap. Decorate it with shells and pebbles.

3

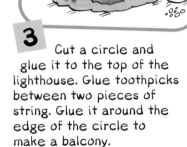

Cut a circle and glue it to the top of the lighthouse. Glue toothpicks between two pieces of string. Glue it around the edge of the circle to make a balcony.

4

Cut square holes in a piece of poster board. Glue the two ends together to make a circular tower that will fit inside the balcony.

Add a fish-shaped soap to your novelty dish

5

Make a small cone from poster board and paint it. Place on top of the tower. Scrunch tin foil and yellow tissue paper into a ball. Add glitter. Place inside the tower as a shining beacon.

39

Glass-blowing

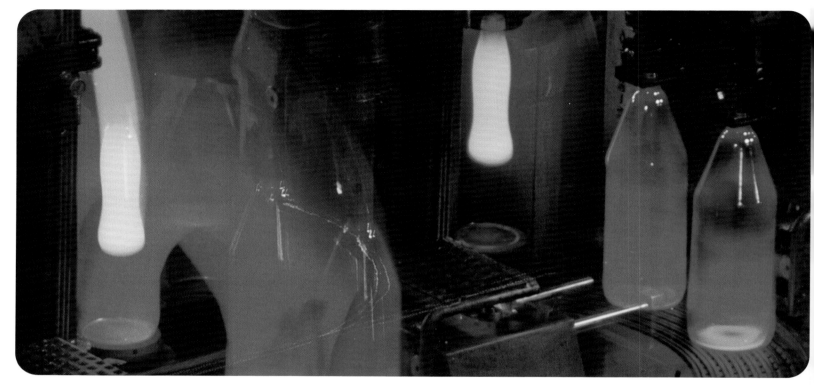

What does the word glass make you think of? Something to drink from? The material windows are made of? We use glass to make thousands of different objects. It is one of the most useful materials in the world and also one of the most beautiful.

Melted sand

Glass was invented by the ancient Egyptians. They first made it about 5,000 years ago by melting a mixture of sand, limestone, soda ash, and other materials. They used the glass for making beads. The first glass containers were made about 4,000 years ago, by pouring liquid glass around a clay mold.

Blown shapes

About 2,000 years ago, glass was shaped by blowing air into it with a metal tool. It was like blowing air into a balloon. Today, some beautiful and expensive glass vases, bowls, and ornaments are still made this way. Most modern glass is made by machines. Sand, soda ash, and limestone are heated in a furnace to a temperature of 2,732°F (1500°C). The liquid glass is cooled into a thin, sticky, material and then **molded** into shape or flattened into sheets.

Flattening and coloring

Window glass is made by flattening molten glass between rollers into flat, smooth sheets. To make colored glass, different chemicals are added to the mixture while it is being made.

Materials

WHAT YOU NEED

small tumblers or drinking glasses

filler paste

large bowl of water

glass beads

palette knife or spatula

Jeweled tumblers

Make a set of colorful beaded glasses to give as a present

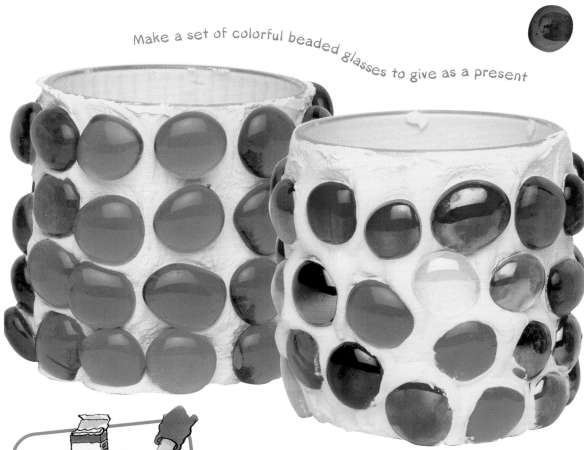

1 Follow the instructions on the package to mix the filler paste. Spread evenly over the glass tumblers, smoothing over the surface with a palette knife.

2 Press glass beads into the filler paste. You can make different patterns with the colored beads.

3 Leave them to dry.

You can use your decorated tumblers as pencil holders.

41

Useful plastics

Colored chemicals

Plastics are **synthetic** materials that can be shaped into almost any form. Most plastics are made from chemicals found in oil. The oil is turned into plastic granules, or pellets, in a factory. Dyes are often mixed with the granules to color them. Some different types of plastic include **acrylic**, nylon, styrofoam, **celluloid**, **PVC**, and polyethylene.

Fantastic plastic

Plastics are very useful materials because they do not rot, rust, or carry electricity. They are also waterproof and lightweight. Plastics are used to make parts for cars, airplanes, and buildings. Plastic nylon fibers are used to make clothes. Shatter-proof plastic has replaced glass bottles and jars. Bright, soft, plastic toys are sturdy and safe enough for babies to play with.

Molding and shaping

First, the plastic is heated until it is soft and runny. Then it is poured into a mold and left to cool. To make it into sheets, the liquid plastic is flattened between heavy rollers.

Toys and toothbrushes, bottles and buckets, packaging and pipes: all kinds of things are made of plastic. Plastic can be any color of the rainbow, or entirely see-through. Some plastics are hard and stiff, while others are rubbery. Harder plastics can bend and stretch without breaking.

Materials

Robot dog

1

Roll cardboard into tubes to make legs. Glue them to one side of the bottle.

2 Cut the top edge from a small plastic container and glue onto the end of the bottle to make the dog's nose.

3

Glue newspaper strips all over the bottle and legs.

4

Paint the legs, body, and face of your dog with a metallic color.

5

Cut out ears and a tail from poster board, as shown. Paint them and tape onto the body. Make wire whiskers.

Make other plastic robot animals, such as a cat or a mouse

Glue on buttons and sequins for the eyes and for decoration on the body.

43

Future homes

What will homes be like in the future? Will we live in underwater cities, under the ground, or even in space? Anything is possible. At the start of the 20th century, there were no airplanes, TVs, or computers. Today, it is hard to imagine life without them. We can only guess at the changes to come.

Eco-homes

The number of people in the world is growing all the time. For this reason, future homes need to be built differently, so they will cause less **pollution** and use less energy. Some houses have already been built to do this. They have **solar panels** on the roof to trap sunlight and make electricity.

Insulation material keeps the heat in, or out, so less heating or air conditioning is needed. Other specially designed houses have roofs that drain rainwater into tanks that store water.

Mission to Mars

Scientists are already planning to build camps on Mars. These will allow astronauts to fully explore the planet on a future mission. An unmanned ERV, or Earth Return Vehicle, will land first. It will then prepare for the arrival of the astronauts two years later. Oxygen and water could be produced on the planet because Mars is similar to Earth. This means less equipment and fewer supplies will need to be brought from Earth.

Futuristic city

- tape
- glue
- styrofoam
- wire
- matchboxes
- pencil
- buttons
- bubble wrap
- foil
- sequins
- small tart tins
- poster board
- scissors
- brush
- plastic bottles and containers
- silver paint

1 Draw three circles of different sizes on poster board and cut them out. Cover with foil and paint.

Attach styrofoam astronauts to wire and make them float above the circular platforms.

2 Cut the bottles into sections. Cut windows and doors from these and from the tart tins. Decorate the houses with foil, bubble wrap, paint, and sequins.

3 Take two plastic containers of different depths. Glue them onto two of the circles and stick them to the base, overlapping to make platforms at different levels, as shown.

4 Glue the bottle space homes onto the platforms.

5 Make space cars by painting matchboxes. Glue on buttons for wheels. Stick on a curve of bubble wrap for the roof.

45

Glossary

abdomens The rear sections of insects' bodies

acrylic Made from a form of plastic.

afterlife Life after death.

archaeologists People who excavate and study the buildings of the past.

battlements The top of a castle wall that has narrow openings along it. Soldiers would fire through the openings while protected by the raised parts of the battlements.

beacon A warning fire or lights.

bolts Short, heavy arrows that can be fired from a crossbow.

Buddhist Describing something that relates to Buddhism. Buddhism is a religion based on the teachings of Buddha, an ancient teacher from India.

canal Artificial waterways for boats.

catapults Machines that launch, or fire, objects into the air.

cathedrals Christian places of worship.

celluloid A form of plastic.

constructed Made or built.

dome The semicircular roof on a building.

drawbridge A bridge that can be raised and lowered.

felt A firm cloth made from wool and fur, or cotton.

geodesic domes Domed structures made up of many flat polygon shapes that fit together. A polygon is a shape with three or more straight lines, such as a triangle.

geometric Made of lines or shapes, such as circles and squares.

girders Beam that are the main support of a floor or frame.

gondola A boat curved upward on both ends with oars rowed by hand.

insulation Protection from heat, sound, or electricity.

levers Simple tools used to raise heavy weights.

Middle Ages The period in history from about 500 A.D. to 1450.

moat A deep ditch surrounding a castle or town to protect it from enemies.

molded Shaped by pouring or pressing into a form, or mold.

molten Melted into a liquid by heat.

mortar A mixture of limestone or cement, sand, and water.

mosaics A type of decoration made from small pieces of colored stone, glass, or wood.

mosques Muslim places of worship.

mummified Dried or preserved to prevent rotting after death.

nomadic Refers to people who move from place to place in search of food, water, and grazing land for their livestock.

ointments Creams that help skin heal.

pagodas Buddhist towers with many stories, usually built as a memorial, shrine, or place of worship.

Pantheon An ancient temple in Athens, Greece.

parapets Low walls surrounding the top of a roof.

plumb line A device consisting of a weight on a string that is used for checking that an upright edge is straight.

pollution The ways in which our environment is damaged.

portcullis A barred metal gate at the entrance to a castle.

PVC Polyvinyl chloride. It is a type of plastic used to make pipes and flooring.

quarries Open excavation sites, usually for digging stone, limestone, or slate.

rafters Sloping beams that support roofs.

sampans Flat-bottomed Asian house-boats with oars at the front for rowing.

skyscrapers Very tall buildings.

sledge A type of sled that is pulled by work animals.

solar panels Panels that convert the Sun's energy into electricity.

square A T- or L-shaped carpenter's tool for measuring straight angles.

synthetic Describing a material that is made by humans from chemicals, not naturally occurring.

thatched Covered by woven grasses.

transparent Allowing light to pass through, so that objects on the other side can be seen clearly.

yurts Circular tent homes of the nomadic peoples of Mongolia that are covered by heavy material and easily taken apart.

Index

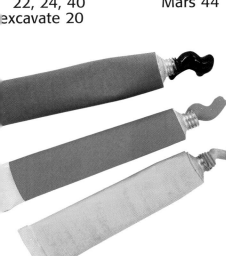

Materials guide

A list of materials, how to use them, and suitable alternatives

WHAT YOU NEED

gold foil

silver foil

filler paste

PVA glue

flour

salt

cellophane or acetate

The crafts in this book require the use of materials and products that are easily purchased in craft stores. If you cannot locate some materials, you can substitute other materials with those we have listed here, or use your imagination to make the craft with what you have on hand.

Gold foil: can be found in craft stores. It is very delicate and sometimes tears.

Silver foil: can be found in craft stores. It is very delicate, soft and sometimes tears. For some crafts, tin or aluminum foil can be substituted. Aluminum foil is a less delicate material and makes a harder finished craft.

PVA glue: commonly called polyvinyl acetate. It is a modeling glue that creates a type of varnish when mixed with water. It is also used as a strong glue. In some crafts, other strong glues can be substituted, and used as an adhesive, but not as a varnish.

Filler paste: sometimes called plaster of Paris. It is a paste that hardens when it dries. It can be purchased at craft and hardware stores.

Paste: a paste of 1/2 cup flour, one tablespoon of salt and one cup of warm water can be made to paste strips of newspaper as in a papier mâché craft. Alternatively, wallpaper paste can be purchased and mixed as per directions on the package.

Cellophane: a clear or colored plastic material. Acetate can also be used in crafts that call for this material. Acetate is a clear, or colored, thin plastic that can be found in craft stores.

1 2 3 4 5 6 7 8 9 0   Printed in the USA   0 9 8 7 6 5 4 3 2

J745.5
ART   Arty Facts.

Structures, material & art
activities /

8.95   4/23/02
CRABTREE